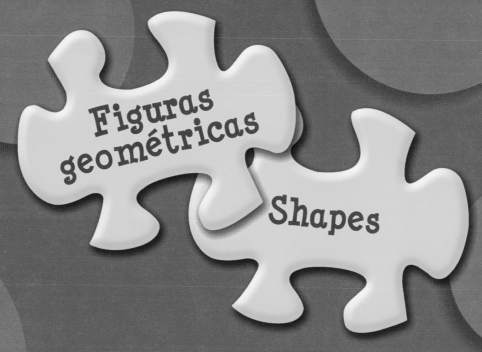

Figuras geométricas

Shapes

Círculos/Circles

por/by Sarah L. Schuette

Traducción/Translation: Dr. Martín Luis Guzmán Ferrer

Asesora literaria/Reading Consultant:

Dra. Elena Bodrova, asesora principal/Senior Consultant

Mid-continent Research for Education and Learning

A+ books
BILINGÜE/BILINGUAL

D1165626

CAPSTONE PRESS
a capstone imprint

Pebble Books are published by Capstone Press,
1710 Roe Crest Drive, North Mankato, Minnesota 56003.
www.capstonepub.com

012014
007934R

Library of Congress Cataloging-in-Publication Data
Schuette, Sarah L., 1976–
    [Circles. Spanish & English]
    Círculos : círculos a nuestro alrededor = Circles : seeing circles all around us /
por Sarah L. Schuette.
    p. cm. — (A+ bilingüe. Figuras geométricas = A+ bilingual. Shapes)
    Summary: "Simple text, photographs, and illustrations show circles in everyday objects and actions — in both English and Spanish" — Provided by publisher.
    Includes index.
    ISBN 978-1-4296-4587-4 (lib. bdg.)   ISBN 978-1-4296-8527-6 (softcover)
    1. Circle — Juvenile literature. I. Title. II. Title: Circles : seeing circles all around us. III. Series.
QA484.S38318 2010
516'.152 — dc22   2009040927

Created by the A+ Team
Sarah L. Schuette, editor; Katy Kudela, bilingual editor; Adalin Torres-Zayas, Spanish
    copy editor; Heather Kindseth, art director and designer; Jason Knudson, designer
    and illustrator; Angi Gahler, illustrator; Gary Sundermeyer, photographer;
    Nancy White, photo stylist; Eric Manske, production specialist

Note to Parents, Teachers, and Librarians
The Figuras geométricas/Shapes series uses color photographs and a nonfiction format to introduce children to the shapes around them in both English and Spanish. It is designed to be read aloud to a pre-reader or to be read independently by an early reader. Images and activities help early readers and listeners understand the text and concepts discussed. The book encourages further learning by including the following sections: Table of Contents, Glossary, Internet Sites, and Index. Early readers may need assistance using these features.

Table of Contents/
Tabla de contenidos

Circles are shapes
flat and round.

• • • • • • • • • • • • • •

Los círculos
son unas formas
planas y redondas.

Compact disc (CD) players read CDs from the inside out. The first song on a CD is recorded near the center.

Los tocadiscos leen un disco compacto (CD) de adentro hacia fuera. La primera canción de un CD se graba cerca del centro.

Circles spin to make a sound.

Los círculos dan vueltas para producir un sonido.

Circles are wheels that roll on the streets.

La rueda es una máquina como la computadora o la podadora de pasto. Las máquinas hacen que el trabajo sea más sencillo. Los coches no pueden moverse sin ruedas.

A wheel is a machine just like a computer or a lawn mower. Machines make work easier. Cars cannot move without wheels.

Los círculos son ruedas
que ruedan por las calles.

Coins are circles you
save to buy treats.

. . . .

Las monedas son
círculos que guardas para
comprarte algún antojo.

10

A flying circle
flips and dips.

Un círculo que
vuela gira y cae
bruscamente.

Pods growing on the cacao tree have beans inside. These beans can be made into chocolate chips, candy bars, and hot chocolate.

Las vainas que crecen en el árbol del cacao adentro tienen unos granos. Con estos granos se pueden hacer galletas con chocolate, barras de dulce y chocolate caliente.

Cookies are circles with chocolate chips.

· ·

Las galletas son círculos con pedacitos de chocolate.

Dolls have eyes
with circles inside.

Your blinking eyelids act like windshield wipers. They protect your eyes from dirt and dust floating around in the air.

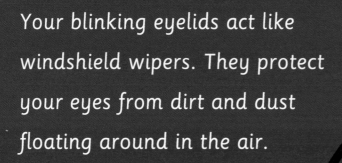

Cuando parpadeas usas tus párpados como limpiaparabrisas. Estos protegen tus ojos del sucio y el polvo que flota en el aire.

Las muñecas tienen ojos con círculos en la parte de adentro.

17

Ride this circle and swing out wide.

Móntate en este círculo y colúmpiate hasta arriba.

Circles hold air
and float on a lake.

Los círculos pueden
guardar aire y flotar
en un lago.

This tasty circle
is a pancake.

. . . .

Este sabroso círculo
es un panqueque.

Candy circles taste sweet and sour.

• • • • • • • • • • • • • • • • • • •

Los caramelos como este círculo saben dulce o agrio.

24

Las papilas de tu lengua te dicen si los alimentos son dulces, amargos, salados o agrios. Pero sin tu nariz no puedes probar sabores como el del chocolate o la sandía.

The taste buds on your tongue tell you if foods are sweet, sour, salty, or bitter. But without your nose, you cannot taste flavors such as chocolate or watermelon.

25

Find the circle that tells you the hour.

· ·

Encuentra el círculo que te dice la hora.

Make a Circle Shaker/ Vamos a hacer una maraca circular

You will need/ Necesitas:

2 paper plates/
2 platos de papel

small cup of unpopped popcorn kernels/
una taza pequeña de granos para hacer palomitas de maíz

stapler/una engrapadora

markers or crayons/
marcadores o crayones

1 Flip one plate so that the back is facing you. Put it on top of the other paper plate.

1 Voltea un plato de tal manera que veas la parte de atrás. Ponlo encima del otro plato.

2 Staple the edges of the two plates together about half way around the plates. Make sure the staples are very close together.

2 Engrapa los bordes de los dos platos hasta la mitad del círculo. Asegúrate que las grapas queden muy juntas.

3 Pour the popcorn into the hole and staple the rest of the edges together.

3 Echa los granos de maíz en el interior y engrapa la otra mitad de los bordes.

4 Decorate the circle shaker with circles and shake to see what sounds you can make.

4 Adorna la maraca circular con círculos y agítala para oír los sonidos que puede hacer.

Glossary

machine — an object that makes work easier; wheels are simple machines; lawn mowers are complex machines.

pod — a long case that holds seeds or beans

taste bud — one of the clusters of cells on the tongue that senses whether something is sweet, sour, bitter, or salty; people are born with about 10,000 taste buds; some taste buds die as people age.

tongue — the movable muscle in your mouth that is used for tasting, talking, and swallowing; the tongue is the largest muscle in your head.

Internet Sites

FactHound offers a safe, fun way to find Internet sites related to this book. All of the sites on FactHound have been researched by our staff.

Here's all you do:

Visit *www.facthound.com*

FactHound will fetch the best sites for you!

Glosario

la lengua — músculo de tu boca que se mueve y que usas para probar, hablar y tragar; la lengua es el músculo más grande de tu cabeza.

la máquina — objeto que hace más fácil el trabajo; las ruedas son unas máquinas sencillas, las podadoras de pasto son máquinas complicadas.

las papilas — conjunto de células de la lengua que sienten si algo es dulce, agrio, amargo o salado; las personas nacen con cerca de 10,000 papilas; algunas de las papilas se van muriendo con la vejez.

la vaina — estuche que guarda semillas o frijoles

Sitios de Internet

FactHound brinda una forma segura y divertida de encontrar sitios de Internet relacionados con este libro. Todos los sitios en FactHound han sido investigados por nuestro personal.

Esto es todo lo que tú necesitas hacer:

Visita *www.facthound.com*

¡FactHound buscará los mejores sitios para ti!

Index

Índice